POETRY'S NOT DEAD

A COLLECTION OF POEMS BY SOUTHERN PUNKS

MILK MAN PUBLISHING

Edited by J.M. Bush
Cover design by Chris Granger @ Southern Fried Creative
Cover Typography inspired by Art by Burx

Photos courtesy of Bobby Lee Hill (pg. 7), Chris Carr (pg.
23), Edward A. McGrath Photography (pg. 35), Reuben
Long Photography (pg. 43), Rachel Gouk Photography
(pg. 53), and Christopher Mathes (pg. 63)

Printed in the United States of America

First Printing, 2016

ISBN: 0-9972842-4-2
ISBN-13: 978-0-9972842-4-9

MilkMan Publishing
914 El Dorado Drive
Dothan, AL 36303

www.eatplaywritetravel.com

To anyone who ever felt marginalized in anyway but, despite that, pushed forward and did whatever it was you wanted to do.

Acknowledgements

This book wouldn't have been possible without the relationships I formed in the music scene over the years. All the contributing authors played some role in the southern punk scene, therefore playing a major role in my life. I want to sincerely thank everyone that agreed to be a part of this project and make a solemn oath to them: One day, I will return to the States and we will have a big ass party to celebrate this book. Beers on me, y'all.

POETRY'S NOT DEAD

A COLLECTION OF POEMS BY
SOUTHERN PUNKS

FOREWORD

P unk Rock means a lot of different things to a lot of different people. Depending on where you grew up, what values were being forced onto you by your parents, peers, and the media, or just how you felt about the fucked up world around you. To me, and many others in the punk rock scene that took place during the mid to late 90's in the American South (AKA the Bible Belt), punk rock was about not fitting in and not giving a shit. We were all different in our own ways; outsiders that didn't fit in with the khakis, the duck shirts, the frayed-bill ball caps, the dip cans, the jam bands, the sporty ones, the popular kids... we were few, they were many. We had blue hair, we had patches on our backpacks, we had cigarettes, we had 7 inches of vinyl, we had Docs, we had shitty tattoos, and we had each other. While the other young folk were lighting bonfires in the fields and drinking whatever liquor they could get their older siblings to buy, we were going to shows and being handed whatever alcohol we could get the older punks to buy. There was a sense of togetherness at these shows. Not everyone who attended was into punk, but they were curious about what kind of music these weirdoes were making. We introduced these people to our world and we weren't dicks about it. And to me, that is the essence of what punk rock was to me at that time.

To bond with each other over common tastes in music is great. To share a love of spiked belts and hair dye is fine, too. But to be true to what you loved, to not give a shit if it wasn't popular, and to honestly try and share it with others who didn't know anything about it without making them feel shitty for not knowing... that is the punk rock I grew up with. It has shaped me into who I am today and I still try to live by those rules. I still have strong opinions and will argue with you over politics, music, movies, or food. I will listen to your opinion and tell you directly what I think about it, good or bad. But now, unlike when I was young, I will respect your right to have those opinions, even if I think they are fucking dumb. The old stubbornness isn't completely gone, though, because I demand the same respect in return. If you can't give it right back to me, then you might as well just fuck off. I don't have time for your shit. And that is what punk has become for me, these days.

I know it's not the same, and that it never will be again. The punk scene itself hasn't changed all that much over the past 20 years. It's still mostly composed of tiny venues with people playing rough music to small groups of very supportive people. But the punk rock attitude *has* evolved, for me at least. Hell, I'm publishing and editing a book of poems. If you had told me 20 years ago that I would one day be doing this, I'd have said, "eat shit, poetry sucks." But now I see it as just punk songs without music. An expression of how we feel about things as we grow older; whether that be political views, opinions on love, theatrical horror narratives, or self-deprecating humor in the form of a limerick. It doesn't matter to me. It's all art, it's all punk, and we don't give a shit if people don't like it. This book is for us. This book is for you. This book is for everyone. Unless you hate it. If that's the case, put it down and move on.

J.M. Bush (aka Milkman)

BOBBY LEE HILL

I t was 1994. I was a lost little kid in a new place with no people. I had just discovered original music when my older brother handed me an old acoustic guitar and started teaching me chords. Within weeks, I had surpassed his ability to teach and was already working on the formula I still use to this day. I had found music and realized that I was meant for it. I considered myself fortunate to have discovered a purpose when I was otherwise feeling so lost. But still, I didn't have a direction. I would try to write but so many influences would block my path. Then one day, I met a guy who would become a huge part of the person I was to become.

Kurt Cobain died that year, and so did my affection for borrowing from the "Seattle sound." I couldn't play any of it with a straight face any longer. Then this guy, Michael Bush, he took me under his wing when I gravitated to the "weirdo" section of the outside break area at school. He started picking me up for school in his shitty, red Chevy Cavalier and we would listen to the most amazing music. Screeching Weasel. NOFX. Propaghandi. The Fallouts. The Vindictives. The Swinging Utters. The list, obviously, goes on forever. I was inspired.

Mike and I started to play around with songs I would write. I borrowed from what we listened to, but the stuff that came out wasn't a copy. It was a fluid. It was blood and sweat and tears, and they were mine. It was real and it was art. I had discovered something which, over the years, I would come to find was... MYSELF. Pop punk changed my entire life. Michael had just started playing bass and we basically put this stuff together as we went. We got some friends to fill out our group, and Michael would eventually name us "Hadji and the Turbans." The rest was small town history and the best years of my life. Hadji became professional musicians *together.* Going from barely knowing how to book a show to worrying about breaking fire codes. It was a blur, but a euphoric one. We helped build a scene in a town where scenes are hard to come by. Hadji played with so many talented people during those years. Blanks 77. A Global Threat. MUTINY!!! The Peeping Toms. Bulletproof. And so many more.

We all did our part to make it last as long as we could and be as amazing as possible. We surpassed our own expectations by far. But, the kids in the band eventually all grew up and spread out all over the world. And so did our music. It's still a beloved piece of the personal history of our little town. The people who love it have shared it with others as they set sail for greater things, going off to live life and build families. It amazes me that it has been 20 years and I am still out there writing music and playing shows. Granted, my pop-punk turned into folk-rock and electric became acoustic, once more. I tried several projects over the years, across the country. I did the best I could manage, but nothing compared to what we did in our youth; just kids having a good time making amazing music.

Nowadays, I always seem to find myself sitting on a stool on a stage, playing songs I wrote using that same formula. The one I came up with decades ago. The one that somehow reached so many people and changed so many lives. The one that carried itself beyond us into a life of its own. And still, there is never a show without someone in the crowd yelling a request for a Hadji song. They look at me with the biggest grin, wanting to hear me cover our own punk music... all alone on an acoustic guitar. I, of course, aim to please, and so do my best to give them a little bit of the past they grew up listening to. After all, it was their parents who were at those broken fire code shows in the 90s.

Finding punk rock music helped me find myself. It is who I am, what I am, and how I will always be. I won't forget the things I owe to those times, and I will always miss the people that were a part of it all. You can put that on my permanent record.

EDITOR'S NOTE: Bobby is one of my favorite people on the planet. He has a laundry list of bad decisions in his past and, to this day, struggles with the effects of them. But his ability to create incredible prose and beautiful melodies makes him one of the most special and talented people I've ever met. He knows love better than most people and, because of this, also knows trouble intimately. He was the lead singer and guitar player for Hadji and the Turbans (1995-2001 – with a few reunions thrown in every few years). He has been writing music and poetry since high school and shows no signs of ever stopping.

Feelings of Hopelessness

Until this feeling of hopelessness leaves me alone
I'll be hopeless and I will always be alone
When this realization of young into old
Settles in, I'll be half way down the wrong road.
Talking in my sleep, I'll tell you all my secrets.

Until this feeling of hopelessness leaves me alone
I am powerless. I can't survive on my own.
When does everything just seem to fall into place?
When you swallow your pride
Become what you ate.
But that's just too much to ask
There's too much on the table.

Things will never be quite what they seem
Time would never allow
I will never be free of these chains
I have figured that out.

When this feeling of hopelessness leaves me to find

Someone else to confuse and control and confine

Every night I lie awake and consider the chance

Maybe I wasn't meant to be right here like this.

Dreaming of the deep end.

Places I remember.

Things will never be quite what they seem

Time would never allow

I will never be free of these chains

I have figured that out.

Five Names

I know you won't believe me,

But I remember all five of your beautiful names

And I hope we both survive.

I hope we find the strength it takes to hold on tight

Because this is gonna hurt,

But I have to say the words.

I don't love you.

Not like you want me to.

Maybe.

Maybe we can be friends.

Maybe I will never see your face again.

And I would pray, if I had any faith.

I'd ask somebody out there somewhere to show me the way

Because this is gonna hurt,

But I have to say the words.

I don't love you,

The way you want me to.

Not like you want me to...

Oh, these big brick walls.

These open doors.

Consequences

Are the background noise.

They are the background noise.

How to Fall Down

Now that I know you,

I wish I never knew you.

You hurt me more than anyone.

I don't want to leave you,

It hurts me so much to have to, but

But you hurt me more than anyone.

You picked me up.

Told me to make myself at home.

Then you would leave,

But you would not be gone for long.

I would care, but not enough to get upset.

No, not enough to make a mess

Of all the feelings we've invested.

You're all I know.

You're all I have

I need you to at least know that.

I guess we know about it now.

I guess we've got it figured out.

Yeah, we know better now

Than ever how to fall down.

You hurt me bad,

Told me I was not good enough.

You would laugh,

As if you found it humorous.

I would cry, but not enough to wet my face.

No, not enough to make a wave

That would destroy our chosen fate.

You're all I know.

You're all I have.

I need you, too. At least know that.

I guess we know about it now.

I guess we've got it figured out.

Yeah, we know better now

Than ever how to fall down.

Love and War

I thought you understood

I thought you knew the score

No one's playing games here anymore

You gave me everything you had

But I needed more

Everything is fair in love and war

Some of them will lie in wait

While the rest of us will charge in

Bleeding hearts afraid to break

But that's okay

It's a chance we've got to take

I bit off more than I could chew

I never meant to hurt you

I don't know my own strength sometimes

It's true

Stay, walk out the door

Do either/or

Everything is fair in love and war

Some of them will lie in wait
While the rest of us will charge in
Bleeding hearts afraid to break
But that's okay
It's a chance we've got to take.

This close to the point of no return
Nobody wins.
Instead of starting over,
Just sit back and watch the end
If we make it outta here alive
We should repent all our sins

Savior

Breathe in easy, baby
How I hope you never have to feel this lonely
So breathe in easy, baby
Now I hope you'll never have to be this lonely

It's a Band-Aid bandage on a breaking heart.
A new day dawning on a dying art,
It doesn't work.
It only hurts everything you work so hard for
Everything you work so hard for.

This cannot be the end of it
Standards fly with full intention
If you wanna know just how I feel
Then come and find me on the battlefield,

And I will fall down on my sword
And keep them all from coming for us
I'll keep them all from coming for us
I would be your savior then, but
It would be too late for us

Hilltops

No one ever showed me how bright it was.

I guess I've never seen the light.

Was it wrong of me to think of how right it was?

Set me loose enough to hold you tight.

I bet you wake up early and you clap your hands,

Drink coffee in your beautiful yard.

And when it starts to rain, you probably open your mouth.

I bet you're even thanking the Lord.

It looks like a picture perfect scene

That's been painted over a few times at least.

And there's a picture painted underneath of you and me

and a storm on the sea.

Yet ain't no hand on a watch ever held us still

Let's make our escape.

Yeah, let's head for the hills

And let the hilltops come between us there, who cares?

We'll let the hilltops come between us there,

I don't care.

About Face

So afraid to make all the old mistakes.
By then it's too late to turn around
to make this about face.
So think before you speak.
I might not know what you mean,
But a "guess what" is too much
to put upon me.

I would be putty in your hands.
I would be yours to command.

The tables turn on ten cents now.
Hearts get called to arms,
The trumpets sing their lonely song
to those who've come to harm.

If life is so short, we must be closer to the end.
If it's the second act then tell me,
Where do we begin?
I say, take this chance and give me all you've got to give.
Don't be afraid.

GINGER ANDERSEN

Punk rock in the south was a last grand stand for culture in America. To be punk rock in the in the American South during the 90s was like being punk rock in the early 80s in NYC. The music was palpitations and each little weird kid was the blood pumping thru the veins under the Mason-Dixon line. It was a movement continuing social change from the country to the suburbs. I felt like punk embraced me when I was 12 and it was my shelter. Finding others in the scene like myself was an unspoken agreement that we shared pains and pleasures without being judged for it. There was a support system of being bold; a discipline in the rebellion; a relationship that transcends time to this very day. The bonds I've made in the punk scene are irreplaceable.

One of my fondest memories was meeting Mike Bush at a Hadji and the Turbans show in Alabama. I was just 16 years old and my group of friends were from a different town not too far away, but going to the city on weekends to see a band like Hadji was the highlight to a life normally camouflaged in peanut fields and pick-up trucks. It was an honest time where it felt like it was us against a world that needed to change. "Punk rock" became all of our lifestyles.

Throughout my life I've moved to many other southern cities exploring the musical subculture their locals had to offer. In South Carolina, I remember Flaming Anus and Steve Hit Mike were local punk favorites. I still keep in contact with one of them and consider him a great friend. I remember writing love letters to Hank III in Atlanta, GA over MySpace, trying to convince him to come by the tattoo shop where I worked. I once had a relationship in NYC with someone who had also lived a similar punk rock existence back in the South.

It was in every facet of my life. Punk was my romance, my friendships, my attitude, my tastes, and state of mind. In these same cities I watched the attitude of punk trickle into other genres like hip hop, EDM, and metal. Punk isn't dead, it just evolved. I think the people who believe it's dead are just stagnated in their own ego and have lost sight of the whole reason the punk movement came about. It was an unseen force that catalyzed change in art and culture. No one knows who started it, or what it really was when it was first happening. You can debate the first band or who coined the term all day. The ends were met by the means of social unrest. Punk still lives. Everywhere. In everything.

EDITOR'S NOTE: Ginger first became public as a Suicide Girl in 2007, breaking out as an alternative model. Her face is tattooed on people across the US, as well as being featured on t-shirts worn by the likes of Kanye West. Ginger has been in music videos and magazines, she's been the subject of paintings and stories, and much more. She is a model, an artist, a writer, and is always in search of her next adventure. We've known each other a long time and she rules. Ginger also makes the best bulgogi in the universe. It's a fact.

The Flood

"There's blood in the water..."

Money trees lynching lovers

Tell me...where is the fire?

Burning and drowning in it Friend of my enemy...

"It's a flood..."

"There's blood in the water..."

Pastures filled waste to the brim

Tell me...where is the fire?

Scarred scarlet stains fading away

Enemy of my friend...

"It's a flood..."

"There's blood in the water..."

Valleys shading the light of your love T

ell me...where is the fire?

I can't love you enough to hate

Friendly enemies

"It's a flood..."

"There's blood in the water..."

Hills full of eyes but lacking speech
Tell me...where is the fire?
There's a war waging inside
Enemies turned friends
"It's a flood..."
"There's blood in the water..."

Ditches drenched in quiet death
Tell me...where is the fire?
Conflicting guilt of appropriation
Friends that turned enemies
"It's a flood..."

Harder

I'm going to make you feel my pain
I know all your buttons
It's just my way of coping
Harder faster deeper

I'm going to push it deep inside me
I know that's where you hide
It's a place that makes you crazy
Faster deeper harder

I'm going to leave you out to dry
I know you'll leave for reasons
It's the nature of my beast
Deeper harder faster

I'm going to make you fuck me
I know you want to love me
It's a shame it'll never happen
Fuck fuck fuck

I'm going to make you get off hard
I know my love will eat you
It's my way of burying you
Just like that

HE:AM

It's April in Manhattan and I'm consumed by darkness
I'm lost at sea locking eyes with the lighthouse
Catharsis cum apathy: The switch flips
Feel these hard tides rip
I'm always almost there but never here
One more day... Wait.

It's May in Philly and I'm burning out bright
I'll tell you that I'm brave but I'm just restless
Confessions masking secrets: The plot twists
The words switch... I'm always almost there but never here
Another week... Wait.

It's June in Atlanta but there was misplaced history
I'm lost thru the sticky summer tears hiding from the world
Lies vs Half Truths: The fingers cross
Keep running thru the loss
I'm always almost there but never here
Another month... Wait.

It's September in Mt Shasta and I'm further away
You're relapsing the repercussions thinking revision
Belief in Trust: The blood boils
Define loyal
I'm always almost there but never here
Another year older... Wait.

It's October in Brooklyn and dreaming abroad
You'll tell me I'm breaking you like brittle leaves
Power and Struggle: The hand is bitten
Once taken to prison in Britain
I'm always almost there but never here
Another moment to wait... But wait.

Weapons

You're further apart than you promised
A balancing act of power and narcissism
My nemesis and lover
My worst own enemy
Loving you is like a painful cut
I hurt myself and you're my knife
Repetition has met its end to a means
Fade out

You're closer than you wanted to be
A breaking point of obsession and hate
Your siren and devourer
Your worst own nightmare
Loving me is like a blunt strike
You hurt yourself and I'm your axe
Impulse has met its end to a means
Drain out

You're around more than you wanted to be

A seduced wave of rest and frenzy

Our failure and reprisal

Our worst own producer

Loving us is like a deliberate squeeze

We hurt and we are the tight hands

Spirit has met its end to a means

Die out

Wrath

Mother may I?
I just want to peel his skin off his body
Vicious, I am wicked
There's no taste like my wrath, baby
I am. I am. I am.

Mother may I?
I just want to pick my teeth with his bones
Twisted, I am sick
There's no touch like my wrath, lover
I am. I am. I am.

Mother may I?
I just want to use his skull as my cup
Darkness, I am rage
There's no sound like my wrath, daddy
I am. I am. I am.

NIK FLAGSTAR

Edward A. McGrath

H i, I'm Nik Flagstar. I was born in Mobile, AL in 1981, and moved to the Florida Panhandle at age six. I was raised by a family of musicians, hard drinkers, and good Xtians on my momma's side and boxers, wrestlers and hard drinkers on my pop's side. Mom is from South Alabama; Pops is from Chicago. They split around the time we moved to Florida. I've always been a musician, as far back as I can remember. I started on piano, went to guitar from there, and then grabbed onto every single instrument I could learn. I sang at both church *and* school. Hell, I was in the Florida State Chorus. I found Punk Rock the way we all should... through a record store. Uncle Scratch opened in my town, and I bought *Nazi Punks Fuck Off* by Dead Kennedys. Afterward, I started going to punk shows. First, these shows were at churches that would let bands play to try and minister to the kids, then they were at coffee shops, skate parks, houses, and then... eventually... finally... thankfully... bars.

My first band was an acoustic Nirvana cover band called The Milkduds. We learned two songs and played at a fair held in a park. After that, I was in a band called The Conformers. I was the singer and it was punk as fuck. Next was The Jamisons, a blues band that dabbled in heavy metal sounds. The next band was called Flagstar. It was an Aggro-Indie band ala Fugazi and At the Drive-In. Ah, but then came my first real touring band, AgnostiA. We put out a couple of albums and traveled around the southeast as far as TN, LA and GA. I played keys and sang (along with two other vocalists).

All along, I was in a ton of other projects: Metal Spike, The Squelch Militia, The 23rd Century, Daigaku, and my solo project. That solo project eventually evolved into my pride and joy - Nik Flagstar and His Dirty Mangy Dogs, which has been going strong since 2003. I've also been a promoter for hundreds of shows in Fort Walton Beach and Pensacola.

EDITOR'S NOTE: I once saw Nik play in a shed. His band AgnostiA put on one hell of a show. Dudes in drag usually do. Nik and I met through our mutual friends Chad Sheppard and Allen Nasty (NFFN, R.I.P). I recall one night, Nik played a solo set at a bar out in the middle of nowhere. As I looked around at the gathered leather and spikes of our mutual friends, I glanced back at the pompadour'd, denim-clad, country-music-playing bastard with the guitar and thought, "that is the most punk rock motherfucker in this bar." He owned the night and I will always remember how great it sounded. I've been lucky enough to play in two bands that shared the stage with Nik; once as AgnostiA, and once as Nik Flagstar and His Dirty Mangy Dogs. Both times it was a hell of a show, y'all.

Drifters

The mimosas on Magnolia Ave bloom almost all year
    through.

Thoroughly, they provide the shade to drifters on the move,

Who walk the trail from way downtown to the store
    where they can buy

Their malted liquor drinks and enough food to stay alive.

I guess it beats a dumpster dive.

The Pearly Grates

16 tons and what do I get?

Another day older and deeper in debt.

I don't have a St. Peter.

There's no where I can go.

I sold my soul to Rock N' Roll.

Making Do

A palm reader's house in Baton Rouge.

A laundry mat in NOLA.

A Mexican restaurant Atlanta, G.A.

A Church in Pensacola.

Underground Bookstore in Athens.

Tattoo shop in Birmingham.

VFW in Biloxi Mississippi.

House show in Alabam'.

NO ONE GOT TO PLAY A BAR 'TIL 1999.

But Punk Rock kids from way down south still Rocked and
Rolled just fine.

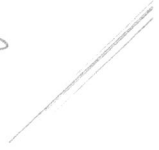

Punk Rock Poetry

1 bowl Hormel microwavable Mac N' Chesse

1 can Tuna in water

1/2 row Saltine Crackers; Crushed

Mix and Serve

Those Nights

It's all about those nights, those nights where there is
      something in the air, that nostalgic emotion.

Those nights where the world feels small and you feel the
      most connected.

Those nights in the summer-time, out of school barbecues
      at a neighbors house, sneaking beers with the
      neighbors' kids while your parents cook dogs
      and you pull the sticks off of bottle rockets.

Those nights where there is just enough haze in the air so
      that the city lights seem brighter.

You and your friends are staggering back from a parade or
      the fireworks and you can still hear the band playing
      Creedence covers from your driveway.

Those nights where your kids can just run free and get
      dirty.

Those nights after a day at the beach where you have just
      enough of a buzz to not wash the sand off.

Those nights in your buddy's garage, tightening the last
      bolt.

Those nights, on tailgates, by fires, that's the answer.

JAMIE DLUX

I was born James David Riley in Boston, MA on Sept 11th, 1980. My family moved to Myrtle Beach, SC in 1991 when I was 11 years old. I've always loved music and when I was young, I always wanted to play guitar. So, I learned how! I spent my teenage years in multiple punk bands and inherited the name Jamie Dlux with the birth of my most notable punk band, Dead Center.

Dead Center was a PUNK/SKA band that toured the Southeast United States nonstop from 1998-2003. We also did a few national tours and shared the stage with numerous bands over the years, such as Hadji and the Turbans, the Independents, the Casualties, the Unseen, the Undead, A Global Threat, Leftover Crack, the Ray Gradys, the Beatholes, the UK SUBS, Maurice's Little Bastards, Static X, Against All Authority, Belvedere, the Classic Struggle, Authority Zero and many, many more.

After that, I went on to play in some other bands and shared the stage with other notable musicians like Hank III (Hank Williams 3), and Wednesday 13 (of the Murderdolls and the Frankenstein Drag Queens from Planet 13). In 2006, I reconnected with long-time friend and ex-Dead Center front-man, Eddy Tanner. We formed my most well-known band so far, SharkLegs; an epic punk rock band who got national recognition for playing and touring with tons of 80's bands... not to mention the fight we got into with the BulletBoys front-man, Marq Torien, at a show we once played with them. SharkLegs is also known as the 2010 Hard Rock Cafe Battle of the Bands winner. We had the honor of sharing the stage over the years with acts such as W.A.S.P., Michale Graves, the BulletBoys, L.A. Guns, Bang Tango, Hookers and Blow (featuring Dizzy Reed from Guns N Roses, plus members of Quiet Riot and Puddle of Mudd), Love/Hate, the Vibrators, Antiseen, Bazooka Joe, the Graveyard Boulevard (ex Frankenstein Drag Queens from Planet 13), the Classic Struggle, the Dogs Divine, Flogging Molly, Skinny Lister, and... you guessed it... many more. SharkLegs is considered active, although on hiatus.

I still live in Myrtle Beach, SC as an accomplished musician, graphic designer, photographer, artist, father of two, and now a published writer! Currently, I can be found playing guitar and keyboards in Sons of Atom, a Myrtle Beach based band whose sound can be described as a blend of punk, rock, pop and new wave.

EDITOR'S NOTE: Jamie is one of the first punks outside of Alabama that I made friends with. Dead Center was on tour and I booked them to play in Dothan. We had a pool party, cooked burgers, and rocked in the middle of the day. It remains one of my favorite memories as a promoter. I still consider Jamie, Eddie, and Jeff (Dead Center) as family.

H.E.L.P.

Half-Hearted Heathens Hire Humanoid Hands

Exploit the Egos, Enslave and Expand

Lie to the Legions, Leach off the Lands

Possess the People in Poles Partisan

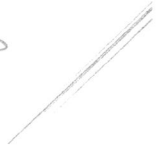

Metaphorical Matrix

a Metaphorical Matrix

a Mosiac Mix

a Myopic Mesh

of Matter and Myths

Multiple Members

Mashed into Molds

a Magical Motif

of Masked Manifolds

Black & White

Checkmate the King - Kidnap the Queen

Revoke the Rook - Rub out the Regime

Banish the Bishop - Knock down the Knight

the Pawns are the People - Robbed of their Rights

2016

Hypocrites, Halfwits

and Hypnotized Heads

Have Mastered the Masses

with Mesmerized Meds

Blinded by Bullshit

and Bolstered with Bribes

Tricked all the Treaters

and Tortured the Tribes

.patterns.

itsy bits of bytes n bots

pixels, points n polka-dots

viral spirals, specks n spots

inking blots n drips n drops

weaves n webs of grids n grains

ploys n plots of plaids n plains

nets n knots, notes n names

patterns of particles, wiggles n waves

The Human Disease

Devour the flower

Topple the tree

Poison the shower

Abolish the bee

Flatten the hill

Watch it all bleed

Oil the spill

The human disease

Balance

I of my center

I of the storm

I the inventor

I the unborn

I of the needle

I of the fruit

I the galactic

I the minute

MICHAEL BUSH

My older brother once handed me a cassette tape and told me to listen to the songs held within. It was Bad Religion. After that, no other music would do for me. I had to have Punk Rock. Go ahead. Ask anyone who knew me in those days about my musical tolerance. They'd probably tell you that, back then, I was the most closed-minded asshole in the world when it came to music. And maybe they'd be right. But this hypothetical person you just asked can kiss my ass. My interests grew to include ska, too! And these days I have a laundry list of musical genres that I adore. But at my core, it will always be Punk. Always.

In high school, I started playing trombone for a punk/ska band called The Whatevers. We were fucking terrible. Cyndi Pappenfus played drums, Chris Granger was on vocals, Steve Capps played sax, a dude named Jamie played bass, and James Davis played guitar. I mean it, we stunk. But it was our first foray into the world of DIY rock and roll. We tried to be as punk as all the bands we had in our vinyl collections; each seven-inch full of energy and righteous declarations of youthful anger. We did not succeed in achieving anything more than off-key warbling and mediocre dance moves. But it was a start.

Jamie, the bass player, broke his collar bone in a very lucky skiing accident. I say lucky because, well, I was assigned to become the new bass player due to his inability to strap on the four-stringed beast. My step-dad took me to a pawn shop and bought me a Peavey Foundation and a practice amp. Wynn sat me down by his keyboard and taught me how to play bass lines. We walked the Blues and rocked the oldies. I sucked, but earned a decent understanding of the fundamentals thanks to Wynn (R.I.P).

One day, a skinny little dude with moles all over his neck started hanging out with me and my friends during break at Northview High School. He seemed like a cool guy, so we invited him to band practice. After we shat out a pile of garbage music, this guy asks if he can get up and play some guitar. Bobby strapped on the guitar and played "Glycerin" by Bush and "When I Come Around" by Green Day. He was good. His guitar playing was solid and he could sing. We soon kicked James Davis out of the band, under the pretense that we were breaking up, and then immediately reformed under a new name. The new group was leaner, meaner, and cleaner. Bobby, me, Chris, and Cyndi banged out the early Hadji and the Turbans songs in a basement and formed the start of the greatest musical years of my life.

We made music. People sometimes liked it. We played shows. People often liked them. Those were the days, man. My roommate Mike Birge and I decided that an album would be the best way to get Hadji's music out there and make us famous. It didn't work. But, with our DIY mindset, we created a record label and sold cassette tapes at shows. Permanent Reckerdz started to get the music we found cool out to the people who didn't have access to it. That venture later evolved, thanks to a large financial contribution by a third party, into a record store in Dothan, AL.

Permanent Reckerdz became the only place in town where you could find vinyl and cds of all the punk, ska, hardcore, and metal bands that the mall didn't carry. We had t-shirts, hats, spiked belts and bracelets, posters, patches, and stickers. We made a little bit of cash from merch, but our main bread and butter... how we paid rent each month... was bringing in touring bands to play with Hadji at shows held IN the record store. The kids of Dothan were EAGER to be a part of the scene back then. Friendships were formed that still burn bright today. We brought in amazing Southern punk bands and made lasting connections with people from different cities. The Metros, Dead Center, Pain, SecondHand Citizen, Dragtime 7, The Lightweights, Leaving July, Ed Temple and the Chalkboard, 7-10 Split... you get the picture. It was immense, it was incredible, and it was ours.

By this time, Hadji was far different than its original format. Chris and Cyndi had left the band ages before. We added Patrick, Lee, and Meri to fill 'er up. We toured, we made another album, and we did what we loved. Being involved in making punk music, promoting punk music, selling copies of punk music, and playing punk music to a live audience is something that built the man I am today.

I don't do much of that anymore, to be honest. I was in a punk band in China for about three years, though. We toured around a good bit and were featured on national Chinese news to 1.5 billion viewers. That was intense. But these days, most of my efforts are invested in writing. Under the pen name J.M. Bush, I have released two novels in the past year. *Storm in Shanghai* is an urban fantasy that has been described as "Harry Potter meets The Da Vinci Code" and takes place in modern day China. *Between the Lanterns* is a science fiction love story set right in my hometown of Dothan, AL and taking place in the not-too-distant future. I was inspired by one of Bobby's (yes, the same Hadji Bobby) solo project songs titled, "In Between the Lantern." Within a week of hearing that song for the first time, I had the outline of a book written. Both novels are available on Amazon, so go buy a copy, ya chump! I need beer money.

After leaving China, I'm now settled in Malaysia for a bit. Not sure how long we'll stay here. The punk scene is minimal. I support the local punks as often as I can. Met up with a cool skate-punk band from Kuala Lumpur called The Tadpoles. Great guys who show that just because you're Muslim, doesn't mean you can't be punk as fuck. Not sure what is next for me as far as where I'll be living in the world with my beautiful wife, Merissa, and our two rad sons, Lucas and Jonas, but I will tell you this... it's gonna be a lot of fucking fun. Oh, there's no editor's note in this chapter. I am the damn editor. READ ON!

Dirt Roads

We start.

It sounds like a melody written in a kingdom from ages long past.

We bleed.

And it feels like a thousand pinpricks given by the wasps of summer.

We pause.

The memory of it echoes like shouts in the grandest of canyons.

We die.

And no one remembers.

Goals

You should always try and be

What you wanted when you were three.

A lawyer, a cook, or a pilot.

A fighter that writes books? Be quiet.

No one said being happy was easy.

And we don't really need a reason

To smile and breathe deep

Or to cry in our sleep.

But the chance to be free is appealing.

So reach out with your arms and just take it.

But, by God, don't you dare fucking fake it.

Or be ready to fight

In the dark of the night

With a big sweaty man who is naked.

Opportunity

She asked me if I wanted to dance.

    Pass.

She told me I should give her a chance.

    Pass.

She once showed me how to be a good friend.

    Past.

She used to say she'd be there in the end.

    Past.

But she died on the second of June.

    Passed.

I watched as her body was entombed.

    Passed.

And I realized I had always been wrong.

    Pissed.

Because she was the one all along.

    Missed.

Won't Goh

See, this life has taken me so far from home
That I'd die for my stance or a chance to be known
As one of the ones who would fight and take a stand
No matter the cost, the people, or the land

Now you wanna start a war of words with me?
That's fine, I won't decline, nor will I flee.
You see, some in the west might think they know best
While some in the east consider we the least

Yet it seems I fall somewhere in the middle, I suppose
But it doesn't truly matter, cuz it's all about prose
And not arguing over the same sad old shit
Though, when the battle to come is the one I'll get hit

So sit back and relax and enjoy the show
I'm staying right here, no fucking way will I go.
Because, I bleed for my beliefs, you know?

JON HAYES

I am a native of Columbus, Georgia and have been writing and playing music since the late 90's. I've drummed and wrote songs for such bands as Strength In Numbers, Ashes Of October, The T Birds (with Mike Bush, the man behind this book), Headstone Hangover, and The Debutante Massacre. From 2011-2014, I toured with The Independents and recorded the *Into The Light* and *Christmas Demo Ep* albums. This was a very surreal experience for me because I started listening to them when I was fifteen years old. Fourteen years later I'm on stage with them. Crazy stuff. I am currently doing vocals for my band Crybaby Bridge as well as playing guitar for another project called Thorns of Rebellion.

I got into punk music when I was a teenager and started going to shows in Atlanta. First punk show I went to was Slick Shoes in 1997. Their singer Ryan was my age at the time, and seeing a kid doing awesome music was inspiring. I went to a lot of shows in Atlanta back then, and still do. I was lucky enough to be on hand when Anti-Heros recorded their live album *1000 Nights of Chaos*. Over the years touring, I've been lucky enough to share shows and stages with some of my idols, including the likes of Steve Zing of Samhain/Danzig, CJ Ramone, Bobby Steele, Michale Graves, Electric Frankenstein, Murphy's Law, and The Heartbreakers.

Punk to me was always doing what you want and staying true to yourself and others. That mixed in with the different types of genres of actual punk music. As I'm writing this, Micky Fitz of The Business has just passed away. I dedicate my poems in this book to his memory and to the lasting music and message of The Business. "WE WANT THE

TRUTH, THE WHOLE TRUTH, AND NOTHING
BUT THE TRUTH! WE WANT THE TRUTH!"

EDITOR'S NOTE: To me, Jon will always be known as Johnny Boy. When we played in the T-Birds together, along with Chad Darkwait (aka Chad Sheppard), I learned how to be in a band that wasn't Hadji. It was a completely different dynamic, and I used the lessons learned with those two dudes for the rest of my life. In the T-Birds, we all contributed to each song, not just in our own parts, but in all aspects of writing. Hadji wasn't like that because Bobby is such an amazing and prolific songwriter. Chad and Johnny Boy showed me how to compose a song as a group through cooperation and communication. Jon was also the first male drummer I ever worked with, as the previous drummers I had played with were both female. This didn't matter too much, honestly. It's not like he was banging on the drums with his dick or anything. But it did mean that, for the first time, I didn't think our drummer was hot.

Early In The Morning

Early in the morning

When the sun cuts through the night

I will roam further down

The valley's warm crimson light

Late in the evening

When the glass cuts through my mind

You will stay silently

In the warm crimson light

I walk the river at night

The smell of her lover fresh on my mind

And I wonder where she'd be tonight

But she's taken away

With the black river's tide

Early in the morning

When the sun cuts through the night

I will roam further down

The valley's warm crimson light

Late in the evening

When the moon bleeds through the pines

You will stay faithfully

To the black river's tide

Early in the morning

When the sun cuts through the night

I will roam further down

The valley's warm crimson light

Fascist Faith

Inhale the ecstasy

Of false realities

The separation of the pure

Towers made of gold

The streets are dim and cold

The separation of the pure

For its will

Your fate

Manifested states

Your hate

Masqueraded as a saint

The serpents won't relent

Their judgment will descend

I'll never bow

Or kneel before your fascist faith

Unleash the prophecies

Draped in hypocrisies

The separation of the pure

Ones that won't repent

Will face the punishment

The separation of the pure

For its will

Your fate

Manifested states

Your hate

Masqueraded as a saint

The serpents won't relent

Their judgment will descend

I'll never bow

Or kneel before your fascist faith

West Georgia Wind

Think of me far away

In my heart, forever you will stay

Think of me now and then

All alone in the west Georgia wind

Whisper things that are true

In the shade, staring back at you

In the darkness there's a spark

Under the moon of Douglas Park

Time is always on our side

The blackest days have withered up and died

I lie in bed and reminisce

Of your smile and of your kiss

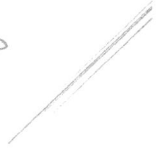

Think of me far away

In my heart, forever you will stay

Think of me now and then

All alone in the west Georgia wind

Permanent Midnight

The reaper's eyes are open wide

Down the avenues where the bodies pile

Their accusations are growing bold

Growing bolder by the day

Watch the ashes engulf the night

Giving way for the permanent midnight

Condemnation is on the rise

Funded by false prophets of greed and lies

Their accusations are growing bold

Growing bolder by the day

Watch the ashes engulf the night

Paving way for the permanent midnight

Spiral South

Pentagram smile with a switchblade stance

Festering in the filth with the rat's romance

The dialect's poison seeping through the walls

Suffocated in agony's jaws

Welcome to deception that spits

Venom like a junkie's last breath

Welcome to impending doom

Claustrophobic, cold sweat, the rage

Tearing me down inside a catatonic maze

Voice of reason foaming at the mouth

The streetlights fade and spiral south

Welcome to deception that spits

Venom like a junkie's last breath

Welcome to impending doom

Spiral south

We are a group of independent artists and, as such, require your help to get the word out about this book. Please post a review to Goodreads and Amazon once you reach this page. It will help put our work in front of more potential readers. Thank you for reading and for sharing with your friends and family. DIY or die.

MilkMan Publishing

POETRY'S NOT DEAD

MILK MAN PUBLISHING

77

THE

END

www.ingramcontent.com/pod-product-compliance
Lightning Source LLC
Chambersburg PA
CBHW060530030426
42337CB00021B/4202